Scripture Confessions
for TEENS

LIFE-CHANGING WORDS OF FAITH
FOR EVERY DAY

HARRISON HOUSE
Tulsa, Oklahoma

13 12 11 10   10 9 8 7 6 5 4

Scripture Confessions for Teens:
Life-Changing Words of Faith for Every Day
ISBN 13: 978-1-57794-923-7
ISBN 10: 1-57794-923-4
Copyright © 2008 by Megan Provance
P.O. Box 701403
Tulsa, Oklahoma 74170

Published by **Harrison House, Inc.**
P.O. Box 35035
Tulsa, Oklahoma 74153
www.harrisonhouse.com

CONTENTS

Introduction

God has an awesome plan for your life. He wants to do great and mighty things through you. He is ready and willing to show Himself strong on your behalf. For those who are willing to seek Him with all their hearts, who will not compromise, who will dedicate their lives to His plan and purpose, a great spiritual adventure awaits you. I dare you to go all out for God, to totally dedicate yourself—spirit, soul, and body—to His service. His Word clearly states His will for your life is success, victory, and abundance in every area. The Bible is full of examples of how God used young men and women to do great things for His kingdom. Now it's your turn.

Everything you receive from God, you receive by faith. A key factor in releasing your faith is the words that come out of your mouth. There is power released into your life when you speak God's Word. It is a vital part of appropriating God's promises and activating the power of the Holy Spirit that will bring God's promises to manifestation.

The confessions in this book are faith declarations based on God's Word. I encourage you to speak them daily over your life. Doing so will help build your spiritual strength and help you become rooted and grounded in God's Word. There is hope, there is help, there is strength, and there is life-altering power in speaking God's Word. Be faithful to speak His Word. Release your faith as you speak, and say these declarations boldly. Speak with power and authority. Release your faith and lay claim to the promises that are rightfully yours.

God Is the First Thing on My Mind

Today is truly going to be a good day. This is the day my God has created and I will rejoice and be glad in it. I am in stride and in rhythm with God's good, pleasing, and perfect will for my life. I will love the Lord my God with all of my heart, with all of my soul, and with all of my strength. I am a child of God and I am made new by His mercies. The Spirit of the Lord lives in me. I am prepared to take on anything and everything because greater is He that is in me than he that is in the world.

May God direct my steps today. May I be alert to the attacks of the enemy and be made physically strong. I am healed, healthy, and whole. No matter what happens today, I know my God will be there to see me through. Today, I choose to let God's love, grace, and acceptance radiate through my life.

Blessings of provision, health, and favor are coming my way. I am not easily distracted but focused, disciplined, and committed to God's commands and plans for my life. I am confident and courageous. I will not be intimidated by the devil, by others, or by any challenge or obstacle

that comes my way because it is God who gives
me the strength to overcome.

Scriptures

*This is the day which the LORD hath
made; we will rejoice and be glad in it.*

Psalm 118:24 KJV

*He was wounded for our transgressions,
he was bruised for our iniquities: the
chastisement of our peace was upon him;
and with his stripes we are healed.*

Isaiah 53:5 KJV

*Be strong in the Lord, and in the power
of his might.*

Ephesians 6:10 KJV

*Christ hath redeemed us from the curse
of the law, being made a curse for us: for it
is written, Cursed is every one that hangeth
on a tree.*

Galatians 3:13 KJV

*Love the LORD your God with all your
heart and with all your soul and with all
your strength. These commandments that I
give you today are to be upon your hearts.*

Deuteronomy 6:5,6

Greater Is He who Is in Me

Greater is He who is in me than he who is in the world. God in me is greater than the evil one and all of his dark forces. God is greater than sin, sickness, and disease. God in me is greater than my lack, my want, and my need. He is greater than any difficult circumstance I am in or will ever face. I rejoice greatly in the Lord that He is concerned for me. Whether well fed or hungry, whether living in plenty or in want, He is the One who gives me the strength to be content.

God in me is greater than any hardship that will come into my life. God in me is greater than any adversity or tragedy that comes against me. He is bigger than my doubts, my insecurities, or any uncertainties. He is bigger than any attack the devil can throw at me or hardship this life will bring.

The Holy Spirit that raised Christ Jesus from the dead is the same Holy Spirit who lives in me. He reminds me and comforts me and makes my mortal body feel alive. It's not based upon my skills, my smarts, or my power but it is by His Holy Spirit that I will succeed in this life.

In all things I am more than a conqueror through Jesus Christ, who loves me. I can face the struggles of this life with boldness and confidence. He gives me favor. He gives me victory. I know that in all things God works on my behalf according to His purpose.

Scriptures

You, dear children, are from God and have overcome them, because the one who is in you is greater than the one who is in the world.

1 John 4:4

I know what it is to be in need, and I know what it is to have plenty. I have learned the secret of being content in any and every situation, whether well fed or hungry, whether living in plenty or in want. I can do everything through him who gives me strength.

Philippians 4:12,13

We know that in all things God works for the good of those who love him, who have been called according to his purpose.

Romans 8:28

No, in all these things we are more than conquerors through him who loved us.

Romans 8:37

The Lord Is My Refuge

The Lord is my rock, my fortress, and my deliverer, in whom I take refuge. He is my shield and my place of security. He is my refuge from the storms of this life. He is my dwelling place, and in His arms I am safe and secure. I find peace in His presence. He is my friend and my defender. His love for me is immeasurable. His heart is *for* me and not *against* me. Even when I have screwed up or I have done something wrong, His love draws me back to Him. His love and mercy are bigger than any sin in my life.

The Lord is my closest friend. When I am lonely, I find love and acceptance in His presence. I am always welcomed to be in His presence. It is in His presence I find rest, I find understanding, I find comfort. He guides me and gives me insight when I am faced with decisions. He is an ever-present help in times of trouble. He knows me to the depths of my being and He still loves me unconditionally.

I am eager to hear His voice and I am willing to be obedient to Him. His Word is flawless, and He brings peace to my soul. His peace keeps me and His grace sustains me.

Scriptures

"As for God, his way is perfect; the word of the LORD is flawless. He is a shield for all who take refuge in him."

2 Samuel 22:31

The LORD is my rock, my fortress and my deliverer; my God is my rock, in whom I take refuge. He is my shield and the horn of my salvation, my stronghold.

Psalm 18:2

As for God, his way is perfect; the word of the Lord is flawless. He is a shield for all who take refuge in him.

Psalm 18:30

The LORD is good, a refuge in times of trouble. He cares for those who trust in him,

Nahum 1:7

Living a Life of Excellence

I commit to live a Jesus-centered life before my family and friends. I am disciplined to focus on the priorities in my life. I can manage the time that You have given me to further Your kingdom. May I be aware of the needs of my family and friends. I have God's wisdom and power helping me as I make these decisions.

Because You first loved me, I am loving, caring, and compassionate toward others. I am calm during times of stress and do not become easily frustrated or lose my temper. If I have sinned against You, I am quick to repent because my heart desires connection and relationship with You. Your Spirit leads me to live a life filled with patience, kindness, and humility. I choose to love at all times and I will provide encouragement and support to those who need it.

I will be sensitive to the nudge of the Holy Spirit and quick to obey His leading. God's presence and peace adorn my life like a beautiful robe. God's grace and favor are crowns upon my head. His goodness and mercy follow me all the days of my life.

Scriptures

If any of you lacks wisdom, he should ask God, who gives generously to all without finding fault, and it will be given to him

James 1:5

We love because he first loved us.

1 John 4:19

Love is patient, love is kind. It does not envy, it does not boast, it is not proud.

1 Corinthians 13:4

Guidance for Your Future

I will obey God's commands and fulfill His purpose for my life. I am committed to fulfilling God's will for my life. The Lord sees my every step and provides guidance for my life. I am full of His wisdom and discernment to make clear decisions. If I ever lack wisdom in any circumstance, I will ask God for wisdom, for He generously gives it to those who love Him. I am not alone in any situation. The Lord has provided me with His Spirit to lead, guide, and comfort me.

God's favor surrounds me like a shield. God is sending into my life the right people, the right friendships, and divine connections that will provide the support and guidance I need to fulfill God's specific will for my life. I am not worried or troubled about where I should be or what I should do. His peace fills my soul. I will seek first His kingdom and His righteousness, and all other things will be given to me. I will trust in the Lord with all of my strength and He will make my paths straight.

I am not puzzled or worried about my future plans. I trust that this earth is God's and everything in it and that He will meet all of my needs.

Scriptures

If any of you lacks wisdom, he should ask God, who gives generously to all without finding fault, and it will be given to him.

James 1:5

Seek first his kingdom and his righteousness, and all these things will be given to you as well.

Matthew 6:33

Trust in the LORD with all your heart and lean not on your own understanding; in all your ways acknowledge him, and he will make your paths straight.

Proverbs 3:5,6

"I know the plans I have for you," declares the LORD, "plans to prosper you and not to harm you, plans to give you hope and a future."

Jeremiah 29:11

Wisdom

The Holy Spirit lives in me and His wisdom takes shape in my life. I am not easily deceived or manipulated by this world. God's truth is deeply rooted in my mind and my heart. I will not conform any longer to the patterns of this world, but I will be transformed by the Word of God. God's Word allows me to call out the lies of the devil and gives me wisdom and insight to make wise decisions. I will be careful not to be influenced by peer pressure, the lure of the world, or the counsel of ungodly people. I will keep my emotions in check, test things, and filter them through God's truth, making sure they line up with the ways of Jesus.

I will seek God's guidance and instruction concerning every area of my life. He is faithful to show me what to do and how to do it. His wisdom comes to me through His Word, the counsel of solid Christian friends, and the direction of godly leaders. God will guide me in the way of wisdom and lead me along straight paths.

Scriptures

Do not conform any longer to the pattern of this world, but be transformed by the renewing of your mind. Then you will be able to test and approve what God's will is— his good, pleasing and perfect will.

Romans 12:2

Wisdom is supreme; therefore get wisdom. Though it cost all you have, get understanding.

Proverbs 4:7

I guide you in the way of wisdom and lead you along straight paths.

Proverbs 4:11

Peer Pressure

I will not allow pressure or expectations from friends to shape me or cause me to compromise my beliefs. I would rather please the Lord than please others. Whatever I do, I will work at it with all of my heart, as working for the Lord, and not men. I am strong in the Lord and I am strong in my spirit. I am strong in my mind to not listen to the lies of the enemy but to follow the teachings of Jesus Christ. Therefore I will not give in to the desires of my flesh. I will not give in to temptation or the persuasion of others to change my values or virtuous standards. I don't aim to please people; I aim to please God. I will not let the disapproval or criticism of other people manipulate me into doing something that is opposed to the way of Jesus Christ.

I conduct my life with honor, integrity, and honesty. The approval of God is far more important to me than the acceptance of other people. I am sensitive to the Lord and I am quick to obey Him. He gives me an awareness of the intent of others who try to influence me. I seek to honor God in all of my decisions, that I would bring the kingdom of heaven here to earth with every action that I take

Scriptures

Whatever you do, work at it with all your heart, as working for the Lord, not for men.

Colossians 3:23

The kingdom of God is not a matter of talk but of power.

1 Corinthians 4:20

Forgiveness

The grace of God is greater than any mistake I make. The grace of God is greater than any sin I commit. God loves me unconditionally. No matter how many times I mess up, no matter how many mistakes I make, He forgives me and loves me and His love is reaching out to me always. He forgives and forgets all my sins; therefore, I forgive myself and I will not condemn myself or beat myself up. He never condemns me, shuts me out, or turns Himself from me. As soon as I ask for forgiveness, the Lord is faithful and just and forgives me my sins and purifies me from all unrighteousness. God is quick to renew my heart and supports me with His unfailing love.

I will not let guilt and condemnation weigh heavy on my spirit. The Lord restores my soul and renews my heart. In Him, I have redemption through His blood, the forgiveness of sins. Jesus took my sin so that I might become righteous. I am made righteous and clean. I am accepted, loved, and appreciated by the Lord. My heart is free from the burden of guilt and shame. The joy and peace of God fill my heart and make me new.

Scriptures

If we confess our sins, he is faithful and just and will forgive us our sins and purify us from all unrighteousness.

1 John 1:9

"Therefore, my brothers, I want you to know that through Jesus the forgiveness of sins is proclaimed to you."

Acts 13:38

In him we have redemption through his blood, the forgiveness of sins, in accordance with the riches of God's grace

Ephesians 1:7

Worry

I refuse to let worry or fear drive me. I will not be anxious or troubled about anything in my life. I refuse to be troubled about mistakes of the past, the cares of today, or the uncertainty of the future. I put my trust and confidence in Father God. I know He will take care of me because He has always taken care of me. I thank God for His faithfulness and peace in my life. I realize that I can't change my circumstances by worrying about them. Jesus said not to let my heart be troubled or afraid, but to trust in Him, knowing He will never leave me or forsake me. I cast my anxiety on the Lord, because He cares for me.

The psalmist David reminds us that God will never let the righteous fall, but He will deliver them. I will look to God and not worry about the circumstances of this life. God said that in this world I would have tribulation, but He told me to be of good cheer because He had overcome the world and will help me to do the same.

In God's Word it says not to think any anxious thought about the future; therefore, I refuse to worry or be anxious about my future. I put my life in God's hands; He will sustain and carry me.

Scriptures

Then Jesus said to his disciples: *"Therefore I tell you, do not worry about your life, what you will eat; or about your body, what you will wear."*

Luke 12:22

"Do not let your hearts be troubled. Trust in God; trust also in me."

John 14:1

Cast your cares on the LORD *and he will sustain you; he will never let the righteous fall.*

Psalm 55:22

Cast all your anxiety on him because he cares for you.

1 Peter 5:7

Fear

I will not allow fear to get a grip on my life. I trust the Lord and believe His Word instead of letting fear control my thoughts or actions. I have the peace of God, which transcends all understanding and guards my heart and my mind. God is on my side. He is working on my behalf. He will deliver me, He will sustain me, and He will give me peace no matter what the circumstances. God has not given me a spirit of fear, but of power, love, and a sound mind. My confidence is in the Lord, whose Word is greater than the voice of fear trying to invade my mind.

The God of Abraham, Isaac, and Jacob—the wondrous God who brought His people out of the Land of Egypt with a mighty hand—will preserve me and protect me. I am not worried or fearful about anything. God is working all things out in my life for my good. I will not make decisions, initiate any conversation, or give any advice based on fear. I have authority in the name of Jesus. God's love sustains me and comforts me. I will not allow fear to influence any part of my life. I resist the attacks of the enemy who would try to bring fear into my life.

Scriptures

The peace of God, which transcends all understanding, will guard your hearts and your minds in Christ Jesus.

Philippians 4:7

You did not receive a spirit that makes you a slave again to fear, but you received the Spirit of sonship. And by him we cry, "Abba, Father."

Romans 8:15

Healthy Lifestyle

I offer my body as a living sacrifice to God in accordance with the apostle Paul's words in the book of Romans. As an act of worship, I praise God with the way I take care of myself. My body is the temple of the Holy Spirit. I choose to honor God by taking care of my body. I will not contaminate my body by eating or drinking anything that causes harm to me.

I am a strong believer, and with the help of the Holy Spirit I will not give in to the temptation of my flesh when it comes to my eating habits. No temptation has seized me except what is common to man. And God is faithful; He will not allow me to be tempted beyond what I can bear. But when I am tempted, He will provide a way out so I can resist. I have the Spirit to strengthen me and therefore I will not give in to my flesh nature. I will not let the desires of my flesh nature control what or how much I eat. I will not eat or drink anything that is damaging to my health.

I will keep my body in shape and drink plenty of water. I will not abuse my body by not getting enough sleep. I will be sensitive to the needs of my body and will make healthy choices regarding my diet and exercise patterns that will help me live life to the fullest.

Scriptures

Therefore, I urge you, brothers, in view of God's mercy, to offer your bodies as living sacrifices, holy and pleasing to God—this is your spiritual act of worship.

Romans 12:1

Do you not know that your body is a temple of the Holy Spirit, who is in you, whom you have received from God? You are not your own.

1 Corinthians 6:19

No temptation has seized you except what is common to man. And God is faithful; he will not let you be tempted beyond what you can bear. But when you are tempted, he will also provide a way out so that you can stand up under it.

1 Corinthians 10:13

I have come that they may have life, and have it to the full.

John 10:10

Finishing the Day with God

I rejoice in the goodness of God. I praise Him for His faithfulness in my life. The peace of God surrounds my life. His peace gives me strength, comfort, and rest from all events and challenges that occurred today.

I will not let my peace be stolen by anything that happened today. I cast all my cares on the Lord. Today is completed and it is in the past. I will not carry any heaviness into tomorrow. I leave any mistakes or bad decisions behind me. I will not let any mistakes that I have made consume my thoughts. God restores my soul, refreshes my spirit, and His joy gives me renewed strength. I am free from guilt, regret, worry, and stress.

I have peace that surpasses understanding dwelling in me. I believe my God will see me through any challenge that I may face. As for tonight, I will enjoy His promise of sweet sleep for those who love Him. I will wake up tomorrow refreshed and restored, full of strength and vitality.

Scriptures

Thou wilt keep him in perfect peace, whose mind is stayed on thee: because he trusteth in thee.

Isaiah 26:3 KJV

(For the LORD thy God is a merciful God;) he will not forsake thee.

Deuteronomy 4:31 KJV

When thou liest down, thou shalt not be afraid: yea, thou shalt lie down, and thy sleep shall be sweet.

Proverbs 3:24 KJV

[The Lord said] I will never leave thee, nor forsake thee.

Hebrews 13:5 KJV

PRAYER OF SALVATION

God loves you—no matter who you are, no matter what your past. God loves you so much that He gave His one and only begotten Son for you. The Bible tells us that "...whoever believes in him shall not perish but have eternal life" (John 3:16). Jesus laid down His life and rose again so that we could spend eternity with Him in heaven and experience His absolute best on earth. If you would like to receive Jesus into your life, say the following prayer out loud and mean it from your heart:

Heavenly Father, I come to You admitting that I am a sinner. Right now, I choose to turn away from sin, and I ask You to cleanse me of all unrighteousness. I believe that Your Son, Jesus, died on the cross to take away my sins. I also believe that He rose again from the dead so that I might be forgiven of my sins and made righteous through faith in Him. I call upon the name of Jesus Christ to be the Savior and Lord of my life. Jesus, I choose to follow You and ask that You fill me with the power of the Holy Spirit. I declare that right now I am a child of God. I am free from sin and full of the righteousness of God. I am saved in Jesus' name. Amen.

If you prayed this prayer to receive Jesus Christ as your Savior for the first time, please contact us on the Web at **www.harrisonhouse.com** to receive a free book.

Or you may write to us at

Harrison House
P.O. Box 35035 • Tulsa, Oklahoma 74153

OTHER BOOKS AVAILABLE
IN THE SCRIPTURE
CONFESSIONS SERIES

Available at bookstores everywhere or visit
www.harrisonhouse.com.

About the Authors

Keith and Megan Provance have been in Christian publishing for over 30 years, with Keith serving as President of Harrison House Publishing for 20 of those years. Together they founded Word and Spirit Resources, a company dedicated to the publishing and world-wide distribution of life changing books. Keith also works as a publishing consultant to national and international ministries.

Their book, *Pray for Our Nation*, has sold over 1.2 million copies and they have authored several other bestselling books including *Scripture Confessions for Victorious Living*, *Scripture Confessions for Healing*, and *Scripture Confessions for Finances*. They are the parents of three sons, Ryan, Garrett, and Jacob, and they reside in Tulsa, Oklahoma.